<u>INDEX</u>

Trump's Publicity

In a campaign-style appearance in Boca Raton, Donald Trump told the Tea Party crowd that he's a real conservative -- he's anti-tax, pro-life, pro-gun, and will *"fight to get rid of Obamacare."* Three elderly people fainted at the rally. We hope they swooned for the April sun, not at Trump's convictions. It shouldn't be a surprise that Trump has latched onto the far-right's birtherism. As he enters his fourth decade as a professional attention seeker, Trump has a long record of saying just about anything that will win him headlines. Especially when it strikes a cultural or political nerve.

It's not even the first time that Trump has flirted with running for office as part of his brand: Way back in 1987, for example, he started buying full-page ads in newspapers in which he opined on national issues. Two weeks after a jogger in Central Park was brutally raped and left in a coma, he took out full-page ads in several newspapers calling for the death penalty for the "savages."

There was another set that ran in the *New York Times*, *Boston Globe* and *Washington Post* (at a personal cost of $95,000) which proclaimed, *"There's nothing wrong with America that a little backbone can't cure,"* according to the Philadelphia Inquirer.

His flack tried to stoke a little political speculation by denying any plan to run for mayor, governor or Senator but added that Trump *"will not comment about the presidency."* In 2000, Trump wrote a faux presidential campaign book, *The America We Deserve*, which Slate's Dave Weigel actually bothered to read, in which Trump claimed that he was ready to lead America towards socialism.

It's worth remembering that 2012 is not the first time Trump's nose for publicity has drawn him into the political arena. But it is rather remarkable that our political landscape (that is, the Republican voters who keep telling pollsters they're eager to vote for a strident birther like Trump) is ready to welcome him. So, drawn from Trump's other political non-campaigns of the last quarter century, here is a history of Trump on the issues.

Health Care:

2000: *"We must have universal healthcare... Doctors might be paid less than they are now, as is the case in Canada, but they would be able to treat more patients because of the reduction in their paperwork... The Canadian plan also helps Canadians live longer and healthier than Americans. There are fewer medical lawsuits, less loss of labor to sickness, and lower costs to companies paying for the medical care of their employees. If the program were in place in*

Massachusetts in 1999 it would have reduced administrative costs by $2.5 million. We need, as a nation, to reexamine the single-payer plan, as many individual states are doing.
2011: *"I will fight to get rid of Obamacare, which is a total disaster."*

The Budget:

1987: *"The fact is we don't need a tax increase. We should have a tax decrease. We should have Japan and we should have Saudi Arabia and we should have all of these countries who are literally ripping us off left and right. . . . They should pay for our $200-billion deficit."*
2000: *"By imposing a one-time 14.25 percent net-worth tax on the richest individuals and trusts, we can put America on sound financial footing for the next century. ... The plan would cost me $700 million personally in the short term, but it would be worth it."*
2011: *"I think hundreds of millions of dollars of money, and let's call it tax money, could come from other countries when we stop them from ripping us off... As an example, we are protecting South Korea from North Korea... Why aren't they paying for this protection? ... So, when you look at a hundred other items just like this, hundreds of millions of dollars could come in, so you wouldn't have to play around with Medicaid and Medicare, and things that are really dear to people's hearts."*

Global Trade:

1987: *"The Japanese, when they negotiate with us, they have long faces... But when the negotiations are over, it is my belief . . . they laugh like hell."* [*The Miami Herald*, October 23, 1987]
1987: *"Let's not kid ourselves. We're supporting Saudi Arabia. We're supporting Kuwait. We're bringing in ships to Kuwait through the gulf. We're losing our men. We're spending billions of dollars. So what's happening? They don't contribute one penny of this defense."* [*Los Angeles Times*, October 23, 1987]
1988: After buying a yacht that once belonged to a Saudi Arabian businessman: *"This country has been taken advantage of by every country in the world, especially our allies, like Japan, Kuwait and Saudi Arabia. So I look at this ship as one of the great jewels of the world, and as an American I'm proud to have pulled it back here. This yacht was considered a jewel, the jewel of Monte Carlo, and I think Americans should have the jewels, should go out and buy the jewels of the world, because we're a great country."* [*The (Canada) Globe and Mail*, July 8, 1988]
2011: *"The United States has become the laughing stock and the whipping post for the rest of the world, whether we like it or not, and we don't like it, the world is laughing at us.. ... I know a lot of people in other countries. I know the top people. I know the wealthy people. They deal with me on a constant basis... They would sit with me at dinners and say 'Donald we can't believe what we're getting away with.'"*

Military Policy

2008: Criticizing President George W. Bush, Trump said, *"He'd go into a country... attack Iraq, which had nothing to do with the World Trade Center, and just do it because he wanted to do it."*
2011: *"In the old days, when we won a war, we won a war. ...You keep the nation, you keep the land, you keep the oil. ... I'm only interested in Libya if, again, we get the oil."*

Polls

Donald Trump has shot to the top of Republican presidential polls on the strength of his celebrity and his bombastic talk. Elites on all sides of the political spectrum – liberals, conservatives, and libertarians – are horrified by his ranting about Mexican "rapists." And he may have shot himself in the foot with his comments about Senator John McCain. But his poll numbers are still up there.

Some voters like his tough talk about illegal immigration. Nineteen percent voted for billionaire Ross Perot in 1992, against George Bush and Bill Clinton, even after Perot temporarily withdrew from the race on the very odd grounds that the Bush campaign was trying to disrupt his daughter's wedding. Voters sense that businesspeople deal in reality, not rhetoric. They get things done. That's why there's always a yearning from someone from outside politics to come in and clean up government.

The website *ThinkProgress* talked to three Trump voters at the Family Leadership Summit in Iowa, all of whom emphasized that point. "*I just think we need a business man to run the country like a business,*" Jim Nelle, a small business owner from Winterset, Iowa, said. David Brown, a farmer and investor from New Virginia, Iowa, noted, "*We're not broke, we're $19 trillion past broke and I believe that he has the business acumen and wisdom to bring the nation back.*" And Bill Raine of New Hampton put it simply: "*He's a businessman, he's not a politician.*"

Unfortunately, just because a businessman understands making deals and building hotels doesn't mean he understands economics. Trump is definitely an example of that. What he's really offering is a mixture of nationalism and protectionist economics along with the promise that he's the guy, the man on a white horse, who can ride into Washington and fix the mess. He dismisses politicians, other candidates, and American negotiators as "stupid people," "incompetent people," and "losers." He boasts of his wealth and promises that he would "kick [the] ass" of El Chapo, the Mexican drug cartel leader who escaped from prison.

He's been barnstorming US talking about crime by Mexican immigrants, starting with his claim in his announcement speech that "they're bringing drugs, they're bringing crime, they're rapists." But there's no evidence for this. Immigrants are about half as likely to be incarcerated as native-born Americans (men aged 18-39 in both cases), and as the number of legal and illegal immigrants rose in the United States between 1990 and 2010, the rates of violent and property crime fell.

You'd think Mr. Trump would be more sympathetic to immigration. His mother was born in Scotland. His grandfather Trump was born in Germany. His first wife Ivana was born in Czechoslovakia, his current wife Melania was born in Yugoslavia. A genealogist writes on About.com, *"Donald Trump epitomizes the American immigrant experience."*

Mr. Trump also doesn't much like free trade. He regularly rails that *"China is taking all our jobs."* He laments that we have *"thousands of cars, millions of cars coming in…They send cars, we send corn."*

At his recent *FreedomFest* speech he complained about call centers in India, asking, *"How can it be that far away and they save money?"* No real businessman would ask such a question. If it weren't cheaper, businesses wouldn't do it. Labor is expensive in the United States, cheaper in India and China. So jobs that can be done in cheaper locations are done there, and Americans move into higher-value, higher-paying jobs. The average American wage is now $25 per hour. Employees in Indian call centers make about $2 per hour, a good wage in India but not one that many Americans are looking for.

Mr. Trump doesn't draw on economics to defend his trade position. It's all about him, the Donald, just being richer and smarter than the politicians: *"Free trade is terrible. Free trade can be wonderful if you have smart people. But we have stupid people. Our trade deals have been made by incompetent people."* He, on the other hand, will *"make great trade deals."* But deals have to be good for both sides. He knows that when he builds a building. But he wants voters to believe that he can just bludgeon China or Japan into … what? Not sending us cars? Not letting us outsource low-value labor to low-cost workers? He'd be hard-pressed to find any professional economist, Democrat or Republican, to serve in an administration based on such nonsense.

This "all about me" approach extends to most issues. The deficit? He's promised to end the corporate income tax, cut individual taxes, and cut spending – but without cutting the biggest programs. How will that work? *"I am going to save Social Security without any cuts. I know where to get the money from. Nobody else does.*

Trump's family

Fred Trump was an old-school promoter, who, in summer, set loose colored balloons near the beach; each balloon contained a fifty-dollar discount coupon for one of his apartments. At his office, on Avenue Z, Fred Trump taught the business to his sons. Fred Trump died in 1999. One son, Donald Trump, took up his father's example, slathered it in gold leaf and topped it with world-class cubic zirconia, cultivated a head of pumpkiny, multidirectional hair, accumulated billions of dollars *(though likely fewer billions than he's claimed)*, and, by the eighties, became the P. T. Barnum of his generation.

For decades, the many institutions of the press—high and low, left and right— have fed off Trump's unapologetic vulgarity, his willingness to say absolutely anything. What did it matter to Trump if Jon Stewart used him as nightly cannon fodder? It was, as we now say, good for the brand. And what is the Trump brand? Over the years, we have been treated to *Trump* hotels, *Trump* magazine, *Trump* Airlines, *Trump* apartment buildings, *Trump* golf courses, *Trump* reality shows, *Trump* University, *Trump* the Game, *Trump* Chocolate, *Trump* the Fragrance, *Trump* Model Management, *Trump* Ice, Trump Steaks, *Trump* Vodka.

But it's always been more than buffoonish entertainment. The sheer number of people and peoples who Trump has managed to insult, bully, and mistreat is, in its way, awe-inspiring. He congratulated Alejandro González Iñárritu for winning numerous Oscars for "Birdman" with this gracious remark: "*Well, it was a great night for Mexico, as usual in this country.*" He once told Bryant Gumbel, in an interview for an NBC program on race, what he thought about affirmative action: "*If I was starting off today, I would love to be a well-educated black, because I really do believe they have the actual advantage today.*" In the seventies, the Trump real-estate company was sued by the Justice Department for racial discrimination in its rental practices in Brooklyn, Staten Island, and Queens. After settling the case with Trump, the Justice Department sued yet again for non-compliance.

In 1989, Trump took out an ad in the *Daily News*, and three other newspapers, about the Central Park jogger rape case, in which he declared that the "*criminals of every age*" who had been arrested twelve days earlier—five African-American and Hispanic teen-agers—were "*crazed misfits,*" part of "*roving bands.*" "BRING BACK THE DEATH PENALTY," the ad read. "BRING BACK OUR POLICE!" Years after it turned out that someone else had committed the crime, and the young men had finally been released from prison, Trump wrote an unapologetic op-ed for the paper in which he called the city's push for restitution payments to the men *"a disgrace."* He made it plain that, to him, their lives were nothing, and, besides, *"These young men do not exactly have the pasts of angels."*

Trump's blithe moral contempt has many targets. He once told *Esquire*, *"You know, it doesn't really matter what [the media] write as long as you've got a young and beautiful piece of ass."* Here's a tweet, circa 2012: *"It's freezing and snowing in New York—we need global warming!"* Trump has been among the country's foremost (i.e., loudest) *"birthers,"* constantly prompting the idea, against all evidence, that Barack Obama was born in some other country and, therefore, is constitutionally unable to hold the office.

Trump is now running for President of the United States. His platform appears, in the early stages, to be a smelly soup of billionaire populism and yahoo nationalism—all flavored with a tangy dollop of old-timey racism. On Mexicans: *"They're bringing drugs. They're bringing crime. They're rapists. And some, I assume, are good people."* Donald Trump is currently polling second among Republican primary voters in New Hampshire, Iowa, and nationally.

Trump has polled impressively, and fleetingly, before. His name recognition is high (*thanks to his frenetically cultivated "brand"*). His moment will pass, the experts say. And it probably will—or, at least, the current moment will. His miserable comments about Mexican immigrants have already cost him business. NBC, which came under heavy pressure from a Hispanic media-watchdog group and many viewers, severed ties with him, as has Macy's, which carried his clothing line.

Trump's political and ideological forays have generally been promotional brand extensions, lasting only as long as they were, in his view, good for business; the whole con might end well before the first snows in Sioux City and Manchester.

William Kristol, the editor of *The Weekly Standard* and an ideologist of the neoconservatives, is quick to say that he does not support Trump, but counsels the Republican Party to learn from his blunt political themes: pro-toughness, pro-winning, anti-Obamacare, etc. Kristol's goal is to avoid the nomination of a mumbly centrist who refuses to attack head on the Obama legacy and, presumably, Hillary Clinton. If the Party fails to find an aggressively conservative candidate, he believes, Trump or someone like him might play the role of Ross Perot, siphoning away right-wing populist voters from the G.O.P.

Trump's Republican opponents seem wary of calling him out in anything like harsh terms. They handle him as they would a live grenade. Jeb Bush, the one

Republican in the mobbed field who is running ahead of Trump in New Hampshire, waited a few weeks before commenting on the latest outrage about Mexican rapist-immigrants storming our southern borders. Bush, who is married to a Mexican-American woman, did say the comments were "ugly," and added that he was "absolutely" offended on a personal level. And yet his remarks, like those of other candidates, were calibrated to assure the public that Trump's comments were "not reflective of the Republican Party." As if this had been a misstep, an aberration, and not typical Trump. Some are unwilling to go even that far. Chris Christie distanced himself from Trump's rant, too, but he was quick to add, "*I like Donald. He's a good guy.*"

Christie is not alone in his affection. Recently, on "The Daily Show," Jon Stewart gave Bill Clinton plenty of room to tee off on Trump. Clinton declined. Trump, he said, with a wily smile, "*has been, believe it or not, uncommonly nice to Hillary and me.*" Perhaps. Not long ago, on MSNBC, Trump said that Clinton was "probably" the best of the four most recent Presidents. Then he added, "*Frankly, had he not met Monica, had he not met Paula, had he not met various and sundry semi-beautiful women, he would have had a much better deal going.*" That "sundry semi-beautiful" bit was an especially, even uncommonly, nice Trumpism.

Hillary Clinton, for her part, could not bring herself to do anything more than tap Trump on the wrist. She told CNN that she was "*very disappointed*" in Trump's remarks about Mexican immigrants—which, considering the fact that the Clintons attended one of Trump's weddings, seems quite polite. But very disappointing.

It's a wonder, though, that Kristol is so concerned. In large measure, when it comes to issues like marriage equality and Obamacare, the Republicans have come through with Spenglerian stir-the-base rhetoric. After the announcement of the Supreme Court decision on marriage equality, Ted Cruz declared, "*Today is some of the darkest twenty-four hours in our nation's history.*" Rick Santorum said that the Court's decision "*put the nail in the coffin*" of the institution of marriage itself. "*The climate is changing,*" the milder Jeb Bush has allowed, but adds, against nearly absolute scientific consensus, "*whether men are doing it or not.*"

Donald Trump is a joke, too, but of a different sort. His intention is not to inspire laughter or relief; his targets are not the powerful. He doesn't punch up. He spews forth ugliness everywhere he goes. It would be nice, and maybe wise, simply to ignore him, in the hope that he will, after all these many years, just go away. But he never really does, and the most immediate concern is not that he will win the office he pursues but that he will get in the heads of the candidates around him. Trump's father was a self-promoter who dispersed discounts in his balloons. The son offers only toxic gas.

Roger Stone

To the extent that anybody can be said to influence what Donald Trump say and do at the presidential debate, it's Roger Stone. Trump's longtime adviser and a former aide to Richard Nixon, Stone has been helping the mogul prep for the debate by drafting policy memos on specific issues and engaging in general conversations about the art of the televised political debate: *"Debates are about themes, they're not about statistics,"* is the philosophy Stone and Trump share, according to a person with knowledge of the mogul's preparation.

Indeed, Stone is just one of many behind-the-scenes players whose work will be visible in the debate, even if they are completely unseen. Whether game-changing moments emerge on camera and how they play online will depend on a cast of lesser-known characters who have shaped the rules of the forum, worked to influence what the moderators and debaters say on stage, prepped the candidates and have their finger on the button of the social media conversation.

Stone is perhaps the most important of them. He got his start in big-time politics as a college student on Nixon's Committee to Re-elect the President, and he publicly embraces his image
as a dirty trickster, including cooperating with a 2008 New Yorker profile by Jeffrey Toobin titled, "the Dirty Trickster."

In the profile, Trump calls his once and future adviser a "stone-cold loser" and suggests Eliot Spitzer should have sued Stone for a stunt in which the operative allegedly called Spitzer's aged father, claimed the elder Spitzer was being investigated for loans made to his son's political campaigns, and threatened him with arrest if he refused to cooperate with an imaginary subpoena. He has a tattoo of Nixon's face on his back.

Stone, who has also worked for Ronald Reagan and Bob Dole, has publicly expressed his disdain for the Bush family and stated his intentions of preventing a third Bush presidency. The person with knowledge of Trump's debate preparation said Stone is not pushing the mogul to lash out at Jeb Bush or any of the other candidates, but, *"If [Trump]'s attacked, which he will be by Chris Christie, he'll respond."*

Whether the moderators or rival campaigns are able to trip up Trump will depend in large part on the work done by Stone and his young associate, though the person familiar with the candidate's prep said the most anyone can do to influence Trump's performance is introduce concepts and information, which he will then formulate in his own words off the cuff on the debate stage. "*He's not standing in a mirror trying out one-liners.*"

Trump's Fortune

In March 2011 *Forbes* estimated Donald Trump's net worth to be $2.7 billion, with a $60 million salary. Many praise and analyze his "success" as if it were self-made, and they fail to attribute the proper credit to others in society where it is deserved. Despite what Trump may espouse, his success would have been in no way possible without his father, the general public, and the US government. Unfortunately, Trump decided to forget or selectively ignore these truths while forming his political philosophy, a sentiment made particularly clear during his brief bid for the 2012 Republican presidential nomination.

Trump was born in New York City in 1946, the son of real estate tycoon Fred Trump. Fred Trump's business success not only provided Donald Trump with a posh youth of private schools and economic security but eventually blessed him with an inheritance worth an estimated $40 million to $200 million. It is critical to note, however, that his father's success, which granted Donald Trump such a great advantage, was enabled and buffered by governmental financing programs. In 1934, while struggling during the Great Depression, financing from the Federal Housing Administration (FHA) allowed Fred Trump to revive his business and begin building a multitude of homes in Brooklyn, selling at $6,000 apiece. Furthermore, throughout World War II, Fred Trump constructed FHA-backed housing for US naval personnel near major shipyards along the East Coast.

In 1974 Donald Trump became president of his father's organization. During the 15 years following his ascension, he expanded and innovated the corporation, buying and branding buildings, golf courses, hotels, casinos, and other recreational facilities. In 1980 he established The Trump Organization to oversee all of his real estate operations.

Trump eventually found himself in serious financial trouble. In 1990, due to excessive leveraging, The Trump Organization revealed that it was $5 billion in debt (*$8.8 billion by some estimates*), with $1 billion personally guaranteed by Trump himself. The survival of the company was made possible only by a bailout pact agreed upon in August of that same year by some 70 banks, allowing Trump to defer on nearly $1 billion in debt, as well as to take out second and third mortgages on almost all of his properties. If it were not for the collective effort of all banks and parties involved in that 1990 deal, Trump's business would have gone bankrupt and failed.

In 1995 Trump took Trump Hotels & Casino Resorts Inc. public and received a substantial financial boost from society and the Securities and Exchange

Commission (SEC) regulations that enable the market to function. He initially sold 10 million shares at $14 per share and then in 1996 sold 13.25 million shares at $32.50 a share. This initial public offering granted Trump's company a stability and legitimacy that would have been impossible without millions of people around the world trusting his organization and investing with the hope of shared success.

Despite the clear societal and governmental assistance described above, Trump continues to be outspoken in his criticism of government. In his book *The America We Deserve,* Trump explains that *"the greatest threat to the American Dream is the idea that dreamers need close government scrutiny and control. Job one for us is to make sure the public sector does a limited job, and no more."* This quote proves to be particularly ironic when considering Trump's feelings about eminent domain laws. He was quoted as saying, *"I happen to agree with it 100 percent"* when speaking of the 2005 Supreme Court decision on *Kolo v. New London,* which affirmed the government's ability to transfer land from one private owner to another for the purpose of economic development in the area. In fact, Trump attempted to take advantage of eminent domain laws on multiple occasions, once even demanding that an elderly widow give up her home so that he could build a limousine parking lot.

Perhaps more disturbing than his hypocritical condemnation of the government is his failure to acknowledge anyone's contributions, save his own, in the creation of his success. At the 2011 Conservative Political Action Conference, Trump made clear his feelings on the creation of his wealth: *"Over the years I've participated in many battles and have really almost come out very, very victorious every single time. I've beaten many people and companies, and I've won many wars. I have fairly but intelligently earned many billions of dollars, which in a sense was both a scorecard and acknowledgment of my abilities."*

Furthermore, Trump apparently sees no benefit in supporting taxes to maintain institutions such as the Securities and Exchange Commission to regulate the stock market, in which he publicly trades his company, or the court system, which actively protects his property rights: *"We are the highest taxed nation—I would tax foreign countries that are ripping off the US and lower taxes for Americans."*

From the moment of his birth, Trump was set up for success. The large inheritance left to him by his father, coupled with the contributions and the protections of society and the US government made his ascension to the Forbes 400 list almost inevitable. Nevertheless, Trump fails to recognize this phenomenon and continues to express his belief that he did it alon

Trump's racism

Under a dark photograph showing hypodermic needles and drug paraphernalia, the newspaper advertisement warned in dire terms that violent criminals were coming to town. *"Are these the new neighbors we want?"* the paid message asked. *"The St. Regis Mohawk Indian record of criminal activity is well documented."*

The ad, part of an advocacy campaign meant to stop a casino from being built in New York's Catskill region, drew an indignant response from the tribe, which called it a naked appeal to racism. The incendiary ads, which ran in upstate newspapers in February 2000, were the work of the New York Institute for Law and Society, an opaque interest group that described itself as opposed to casino gambling.

Long before Mr. Trump announced his bid for the Republican presidential nomination, roiling the 2016 election with his pugnacious style and speeches in which he has branded many undocumented immigrants as rapists and murderers, he had proved himself in New York as an expert political provocateur with an instinct for racially charged rhetoric.

To communities that have clashed with Mr. Trump in the past, his current strategy is entirely familiar. The slash-and-burn offensive against casino gambling in New York was a revealing foray into local politics, but it was only one of several episodes that seem to foreshadow the tone of his presidential campaign.

In 1989, amid a citywide panic in New York prompted by the assault of a white female jogger in Central Park, Mr. Trump ran advertising that called for a return of the death penalty. Later, during negotiations with the town of Palm Beach, Fla., his associates threatened through the media to sell a beachfront estate owned by Mr. Trump to the Unification Church, a Christian sect founded in South Korea and known for the practice of holding mass weddings.

Mr. Trump acknowledged that his style can be offensive to some, but he defended it as essential for communicating his message. *"It would be nice to be somewhat gentler,"* he said in an interview this week, *"but at the same time, I don't think I would be able to make the point nearly as well, whether it's the death penalty or other things, totally unrelated."*

Mr. Trump said it was "not my intention" to speak in racially provocative terms, but expressed little interest in softening his language. *"It's very time-consuming to be politically correct,"* he said, *"and I don't like wasting a lot of time."*

He has used divisive rhetoric to advance his business interests: His drive against the St. Regis Mohawks was intended to protect his investments in Atlantic City at the time, by blocking casino development in a competing market. Mr. Trump, who stood by the content of the newspaper and television ads he paid for, said he had made a *"tremendous amount of money in Atlantic City"* and did not want to see gamblers migrating elsewhere.

"I wasn't knocking the Mohawks; I was knocking their record," Mr. Trump said. *"That's not because they're Mohawks. That's because their record is bad and was proved to be bad at the time."* The ads shocked local tribal leaders, who took out their own newspaper ad in response to denounce the "racist and inflammatory rhetoric of this sham Institute. *"How dare they smear a nation and brand us all as criminals,"* the ad said.

The anti-St. Regis ads drew the scrutiny of New York's lobbying commission, and Mr. Trump acknowledged that he was the New York Institute for Law and Society's primary sponsor. In a settlement with the state, he and his advisers agreed to pay a fine and run a set of ads apologizing, not for the content of the anti-Mohawk ads, but for evading state disclosure rules related to lobbying and political advocacy.

The new ads expressed regret *"if anyone was misled concerning the production and funding of the lobbying effort,"* according to settlement documents obtained through a state records request. Rowena General, who was chief of staff for the St. Regis Mohawks in 2000, said Mr. Trump's ad campaign was a cynical attempt to use fear about race and crime to protect his business investments. The tenor of his presidential campaign, she said, was *"not surprising at all, considering our experience with him."*

Eleven years earlier, Mr. Trump had financed what was perhaps an even more charged advertisement days after the brutal assault on the jogger in Central Park. The ad, in the form of an open letter from Mr. Trump, was topped with two sentences that blared: *"Bring Back the Death Penalty. Bring Back Our Police!"*

The message, which appeared in four publications, including The New York Times, channeled widespread anger and fear about violent crime. Invoking the image of "roving bands of wild criminals" wreaking havoc on the streets, Mr. Trump's letter rebuked Mayor Edward I. Koch, a Democrat who supported the death penalty, for urging New Yorkers not to turn to hate in the aftermath of the Central Park assault.

"I want to hate these muggers and murderers," Mr. Trump wrote in the ad. *"They should be forced to suffer and, when they kill, they should be executed for their crimes."*

The rape and near-murder in Central Park rocked New York in the midst of the 1989 mayoral race, becoming a chilling symbol of a city seemingly out of control. Over time, it also came to represent the flaws in the criminal justice system. Five teenagers, four of them black, one Latino, were arrested and imprisoned for carrying out the attack. Known as the Central Park Five, they had their convictions vacated years later after another man, Matias Reyes, confessed to the crime.

State Senator Bill Perkins, a Democrat who at the time was president of the tenants' association at Schomburg Plaza, the Manhattan apartment complex where several of the defendants lived, said he was horrified to see Mr. Trump emerge as a contender for the presidency. A framed copy of Mr. Trump's 1989 newspaper ad hangs in Mr. Perkins's Harlem office as a reminder, he said, of an ugly moment in the city's recent past.

This was taking a moment, a very unfortunate and one might say racially tense moment in our city, and fueling a lynch mob," Mr. Perkins, who is black, said of the ad. *"This is the* <u>Donald Trump</u> *that we have to remember as we pay attention to his ranting, his continuous ranting and carrying on."*

Mr. Trump said that the ad was motivated purely by his support for reinstituting the death penalty and that it did not have a racial component. He said he remained a strong proponent of capital punishment and called it a necessary deterrent to violent crime. *"This had nothing to do with race,"* he said. *"I have always been a big believer, and continue to be, of the death penalty for horrendous crime."*

He added that he had no regrets about the ad, though he noted that because the victim of the assault had survived, the death penalty would not have been appropriate. New York City last year settled a lawsuit brought by the five defendants for $41 million, without acknowledging wrongdoing.

Jonathan C. Moore, a lawyer who represents four of the men, said Mr. Trump had shown an *"incredible lack of judgment"* in the Central Park case. His clients, Mr. Moore said, had been in the park on the night of the attack but had committed no crime.

"Donald Trump was an example of how, mostly white people, rushed to judgment about what happened there," said Mr. Moore, who is white. Describing the victim and her alleged attackers, he added, *"It was a young white investment banker, and all these young black kids who looked like they were guilty."*

Even now, Mr. Trump refuses to completely back down. He criticized the city's settlement, arguing that the young men had been convicted by a jury and had probably been involved in some kind of criminal activity on the night of the assault.

"They walked away with $41 million and the best thing they had going for them was they were wilding in other parts of the park, beating the hell out of people," Mr. Trump said, using a term, popularized after the Central Park assault, for young men going on a crime spree.

Two years after running the ads about the Central Park case, Mr. Trump drew accusations of racism during a lobbying effort in Palm Beach, where he was seeking to subdivide the palatial estate known as Mar-a-Lago. As he faced considerable opposition from the town, articles appeared almost simultaneously in both The New York Post and The Palm Beach Daily News reporting, based on anonymous sources, that he might sell the property to the Unification Church.

The church, which was founded by the Rev. Sun Myung Moon and viewed by many at the time as a cult, roundly denied any interest in the property and accused Mr. Trump of using the faith as a racial and religious cudgel against officials in the Florida town. Dr. James A. Baughman, who led the church's branch in the United States at the time, said then that the church had no interest in the property. Mr. Trump, he said, was using "the Unification Church as a scare tactic in an attempt to compel Palm Beach officials to submit to the will of Mr. Trump."

The town ultimately rejected Mr. Trump's bid to subdivide the estate, and he converted it to a private club instead. He said this week that any suggestion the property would be sold to the Unification Church "certainly wasn't intended" to be racial in nature. Indeed, Mr. Trump sounded incredulous at the notion. "That's Korean," he said of the church. *"So now I'm against the Koreans, too, you mean?"*

In the presidential campaign, Mr. Trump has discussed crime and immigration in explicitly alarmist terms. He has highlighted murders committed by undocumented immigrants, and has repeatedly referred to an undocumented

Mexican immigrant who has been charged with killing a young woman in San Francisco as "this animal."

The furor over his comments led NBC to sever its ties with him: He will no longer be associated with the "Apprentice" franchise, and NBC's parent, NBC Universal, said the network would no longer carry the Miss USA and Miss Universe pageants, part of a joint venture with Mr. Trump.

He said that there might be some value in speaking with greater restraint, but that that would exact its own price: *"I might not get my point across nearly as well."* "The interesting thing is," he said, *"I am probably the least racist person that you will ever speak to."*

Even as a downward spiral drags down his business interests and presidential ambitions, Donald Trump has ignored virtually every possible chance to walk back his deeply offensive remarks about Mexican immigrants. Instead — just like lies — each time Trump has repeated his most damning assertions, they have only grown bigger and even more unwieldy.

First he called Mexicans drug dealers and rapists. Then they were killers, too. He accused the Mexican government of forcing Univision out of a broadcasting Miss USA and Miss Universe. Trump claims that was totally his idea. He has suggested that Middle Eastern terrorists have illegally crossed the U.S.-Mexico border. Don't worry, none of this is offensive, Trump says, because he *"loves the Mexican people"* and *"the Latinos love Trump."*

For what it's worth, Trump's claims are not accurate. Very little fact-checking is needed to see that his words are both out of touch and inflammatory. And in a sense, that's on par with his reputation. He has branded his entire public persona as a brash, attention-hungry mogul willing to toe the line of controversy for a few ounces of free publicity. Trump has teased the prospect of a presidential run for years, and now that he's officially in the race, his time has come to revel in the attention — whether it be positive or negative.

And even if general election voters don't take Trump seriously as a viable GOP candidate, he's bound to have a dramatic effect on the framing of the immigration debate. It's an issue already dogging Republicans and one bound to remain a major issue throughout the 2016 election. When mainstream candidates take the stage for their first-ever primary debate of this election, it's likely that Trump will be standing next to them, fielding the uncomfortable but genuine questions over how Republicans expect to make inroads with Latino voters in light of the harsh anti-immigrant rhetoric.

For some GOP candidates, Trump's decision to throw political-correctness into the wind would be welcomed addition to the immigration debate. Any position against legal immigration or a pathway to citizenship or subtly divisive rhetoric is nowhere near as extreme as Trump's comments. His controversy is now sucking up all the oxygen on the issue, leaving aside conversation on the substantive aspects of immigration platforms that could be seen as problematic come the general election.

Texas Sen. Ted Cruz, whose father is Cuban, even defended the real estate mogul and condemned NBC Universal for its "political correctness" in dropping Trump from the Miss USA and Miss Universe pageants.

Few 2016 presidential candidate in the GOP field have denounced Trump's remarks. Former Florida Gov. Jeb Bush, whose wife is from Mexico and whose children are Mexican-American, addressed the issue after a campaign speech in Nevada, notably speaking in Spanish for those directly impacted to hear, while lost in translation for others in the base who might not agree.

"*I do not agree with his words*," Bush said in Spanish during a campaign event in Nevada. "*They do not represent the values of the Republican Party and they do not represent my values.*" Former New York Gov. George Pataki came out forcefully against Trump, calling his remarks clearly "disrespectful."

The silence from the rest of the crowded GOP field has been deafening in the two weeks since Trump entered the race. It's an interesting development considering the direction that the nation is heading. A new study out by the Pew Research Center last week found that the U.S. Hispanic population has reached a new high of 55.4 million people. While the rate of the country's Hispanic growth has started to cool, Latinos now make up more than 17% of the U.S. population.

The growth marks a dramatic shift in the nation's demographics with minority groups projected to soon make up the majority of Americans, forever reshaping U.S. politics and political parties' pathways to the presidency.

A separate Pew study shows, however, what a sticky situation immigration can be for Republican candidates. Some 63% of Republican voters said they view immigrants as a "burden" for sucking up all of America's jobs, housing and health care.

For a party trying desperately to shed its disastrous 2012 "self-deportation" platform on immigration, Republicans are still struggling to take a more welcoming tack toward a nation of immigrants. Candidates this election cycle have already seen how much of a balancing act any discussion on immigration can be, as they attempt to appeal to their base without alienating one of the fastest growing groups in the country. If Trump's devolving controversy is any indication, it's an issue that will only continue to be a problem for Republicans — unless they change course.

Donald Trump is no Republican sideshow, the country's largest Latino advocacy organization is warning. He's a real, potentially long-term hindrance to the party's chances of capturing any significant portion of the Hispanic vote in 2016's presidential election.

That's the message Janet Murguía, the leader of the National Council of La Raza, sent in an interview and labeled the presidential candidate's remarks about Mexican immigrants, "by definition, racism."

In a speech to an audience of Hispanic activists that heard Democratic presidential candidates Hillary Clinton, Bernie Sanders and Martin O'Malley pitch themselves while they criticized Trump, Murguía plans to call on Republican leaders and candidates to aggressively repudiate Trump's statement — and reiterations — that Mexican immigrants are "bringing drugs, they're bringing crime, they're rapists," according to an advance copy of the speech.

"To the leadership of the Republican Party and its candidates for president, I have this to say: What's your excuse?" she asked. *"The clock is ticking. Trump keeps doubling down."* The stark warning sent by the former Clinton administration official whose group has previously hosted Republican presidents — including George H.W. Bush and George W. Bush — came as Trump climbs in national and early-state polls. His shadow looms over the annual convention of the generally left-leaning grass-roots group that supports immigration reform, a convention that saw no Republican candidates in attendance this year.

While Democrats have universally decried Trump's comments — and used them to portray the Republican Party as a backward and bigoted institution — some Republicans have been far more cautious, eyeing the candidate's rising poll numbers as evidence of actual support on the ground for his message.

The message sent by the influential Latino group is unlikely to immediately sway large swaths of GOP leadership, but it puts further pressure on a party that has struggled to relate to the crucial voting bloc in recent years.

Murguía said she has not heard from any Republican leader since Trump entered the race with a strict anti-illegal immigration message, and other candidates — including Jeb Bush — declined invitations to Kansas City.

GOP leaders' refusal to repudiate Trump weighs more heavily on the party every day as it strays further from its post-2012 report outlining a path to reconciling with Latino voters, Murguía said, though she does plan to acknowledge Bush and Sen. Lindsey Graham as two candidates who have distanced themselves from Trump in her address.

Pointing to businesses that have severed ties with the billionaire and name-checking Republican leaders who made controversial but principled choices for minority groups — from Abraham Lincoln, to Ronald Reagan, to Nikki Haley — the Hispanic leader made the case that there is an easy way for GOP members to show Latino voters that they care.

"Are they so afraid of the 'Trump wing' of the party that they're willing to pass up a chance to make their case to the nation's largest ethnic minority and its fastest-growing group of voters?" she asked. *"They're perilously close to really damaging their brand with Latino voters, and time is not their friend,"* she said in a back room of the sprawling convention center hosting the conference. *"The longer this goes, the more difficult and damaging it is with the Latino vote."*

After Barack Obama was reelected in 2012 the Republican National Committee commissioned a so-called autopsy report that eventually outlined ways for the party to climb back into the White House. A top priority was appealing to Hispanic voters, but many of its recommended steps for doing so — like embracing comprehensive immigration reform — have fallen by the wayside.

"What's so remarkable here is they wrote their own playbook about what went wrong and what they needed to do to fix it with the Latino electorate after the poor showing by candidate Romney last time," Murguía said. *"And yet, it feels like at every turn they have ignored it, walked away from it, refused to follow it, and it's hard to know why. Because they actually did have a good plan when they had that autopsy."*

The recent dustup over Trump's comments has seen Democratic candidates push immigration reform particularly strongly on the campaign trail, further drawing contrasts by portraying Trump as a de facto spokesman for his party.

"The real problem isn't that the Republicans have such a hate-spewing character running for president — the problem is that it's so hard to tell him apart from other candidates," said O'Malley, the former Maryland governor.

"I don't have to wait to become president to take a stand right here, right now, against the divisive rhetoric that demonizes immigrants and their families,"

Clinton said. Still, Murguía said, even if the controversy helps elect a pro-immigration reform Democrat, if there is no clean resolution within the Republican Party, longer-term fixes to the immigration debate are unlikely to come anytime soon

"When one party is AWOL in a presidential election as it relates to a significant voting bloc, it's not good for us at the end of the day, to get those permanent solutions that we need," she explained. *"It's a bad sign for the future of the country if the parties are not showing up to engage voters directly."*

Trump's misogyny

For decades, Donald Trump has made flippant misogyny as much a part of his trademark as his ostentatious lifestyle. Now, the former reality-television host and current front-runner in the polls for the 2016 GOP presidential nomination may be paying a price for a boorish barb that also renewed his party's internal consternation over its recent history of alienating women voters.

What did it was not what he said — which was in keeping with his earlier comments — but directing it at a highly regarded Fox News Channel anchor who is popular with the Republican faithful.

Trump was disinvited to speak at Saturday's RedState Gathering of conservative activists in Atlanta after the celebrity real estate mogul seemed to hint that Megyn Kelly's menstrual cycle drove her to ask him tough questions at Thursday night's Republican debate in Cleveland.

"I think there is a line of decency that even a nonprofessional politician can cross. Suggesting that a female journalist asking you a hostile question is hormone-related, I think, is one of those lines," conference organizer Erick Erickson said in an interview.

Yet Trump has a history of similar inflammatory statements about women — both as a sex, and with reference to his antagonists and subordinates. As far back as a 1991 interview with Esquire magazine, Trump had boasted: *"You know, it doesn't really matter what [the media] write as long as you've got a young and beautiful piece of [expletive]. But she's got to be young and beautiful."*

In a 2006 book, he wrote of women as objectified collectibles: *"Beauty and elegance, whether in a woman, a building, or a work of art is not just superficial or something pretty to see."* He once sent New York Times columnist Gail Collins a copy of something she had written about him with her picture circled and "The face of a dog!" written over it.

And in 2012, he tweeted that Huffington Post founder Arianna Huffington is *"unattractive both inside and out. I fully understand why her former husband left her for a man — he made a good decision."* In debate, moderator Kelly reprised other Trump comments. "You've called women you don't like fat pigs, dogs, slobs, and disgusting animals,'" she said.

"Your Twitter account has several disparaging comments about women's looks," Kelly continued. *"You once told a contestant on 'Celebrity Apprentice' it would be a pretty picture to see her on her knees. Does that sound to you like the temperament of a man we should elect as president, and how will you answer the charge from Hillary Clinton, who [is] likely to be the Democratic nominee, that you are part of the war on women?"*

Trump replied that he was battling a greater scourge — political correctness — and *"frankly, what I say, and oftentimes it's fun, it's kidding. We have a good time."*

Then, he issued what sounded like a threat: *"Honestly Megyn, if you don't like it, I'm sorry. I've been very nice to you, although I could probably maybe not be, based on the way you have treated me. But I wouldn't do that."*

On Friday, Trump did exactly that. He retweeted a Twitter follower's description of Kelly as a "bimbo," and told CNN that Kelly *"had blood coming out of her eyes, blood coming out of her wherever."* Later, Trump's campaign issued a statement maintaining that he had been referring to Kelly's nose, not her hormonal cycle, and that *"only a deviant would think anything else."*

The comment was *"completely in character for Trump,"* said Katie Packer Gage, a political consultant who was GOP nominee Mitt Romney's deputy campaign manager in 2012. *"What's new is he picked on somebody who is beloved by conservative voters, and he has just doubled and tripled down on it."*

His rivals warn that Trump's comments about women will reflect badly on the entire party.

"Give me a break. Do we want to win? Do we want to insult 53 percent of all voters? What Donald Trump said is wrong," former Florida governor Jeb Bush said during his appearance at the RedState event. *"Mr. Trump ought to apologize."*

Instead, the real estate mogul ramped up his criticism of Kelly in an interview with The Washington Post: *"She's a lightweight as a reporter, very unprofessional. Her questions were ridiculous."*

It remains to be seen how much — if at all — the episode has damaged Trump's standing. His earlier comments characterizing illegal immigrants as rapists and killers, and disparaging the military service of Sen. John McCain (R-Ariz.) might also have been fatal to another candidacy, but only seemed to draw more supporters to Trump.

Polls to date not only show him with a strong lead over the other 16 Republican contenders, but that among GOP primary voters, women are nearly as likely to support him as men are.

In part, that is because he is running as a celebrity outsider who gives voice to the frustrations that many voters feel with the political system. Trump, however, will be given more scrutiny as voters get closer to making a decision at the polls.

"What's different is that nobody ever focused or heard any of those comments through the lens of a man who wants to be president," said Republican pollster Kellyanne Conway, who is working for a super PAC supporting the candidacy of Sen. Ted Cruz (R-Tex.). *"In the past, he's been a businessman, the host of a popular program."*

Trump's greater challenge, over the long term, might have been demonstrated during other, less-talked-about segments of Thursday's debate, which was the first of nine officially sanctioned face offs that are scheduled during the primary season. Pressed repeatedly for evidence to back up some of his more outlandish claims — such as that the Mexican government was dispatching murderers and rapists across the border — Trump was vague and evasive. Nor has he come up with much by way of policy prescriptions, beyond suggesting that the force of his own personality is the answer to the nation's problems.

Why Donald Trump Matters

Now that Donald Trump is in the race, it's time to stop thinking of him as a joke. The tossed-off braggadocio, like this line from Tuesday's announcement: *"I will be the greatest jobs president that God ever created. I tell you that."* Or the "huh?" lines: *"We have to repeal Obamacare, and it can be—and—and it can be replaced with something much better for everybody."* And then there's the stuff about Barack Obama's citizenship.

Trump matters now and not for the reasons that have already been cited: his net worth, a self-reported $8.5 billion, or his capacity to edge a Rick Perry or John Kasich out of the 10 slots open for the first presidential debate.

Trump matters because promoting two ideas that are in sync with today's GOP—being tough on trade and opposing cuts in entitlements—gives him (or a more palatable messenger) some real potential. As white working-class voters have migrated to the Republican Party, they've brought their tough-on-trade views with them. A Pew study last month found Republicans to be more skeptical of trade agreements than Democrats are and more likely to believe they have cost jobs.

But the presidential candidates have free trade records—reflecting the legacy of their party, not its new blue-collar migrants. Trump more or less has the tough-on-trade field to himself. Jeb Bush, Ted Cruz, Marco Rubio and Scott Walker favor fast-track authority for the Trans-Pacific Partnership. Trump denounces it.

Mike Huckabee has been a notable exception—his line from 2008 about how China "Shanghaied" our economy is Trumpesque—but trade is not one of his leading issues, whereas Trump made it the centerpiece of his announcement, hurling barbs at Beijing and fellow Republicans within the first moments of his announcement speech. *"I hear their speeches. They don't talk jobs. When was the last time you heard them talk about China?"* Trump said. *"You don't hear it from anyone else."*

Likewise, when it comes to cutting entitlements, while candidates like Chris Christie and Rubio have talked about entitlement reforms, Trump has consistently said that they shouldn't be cut, and he repeated that claim in his announcement speech. Polls show that Republicans are adamantly opposed to entitlement cuts, albeit at somewhat lower levels than Democrats.

The demographic shifts in support of the Republican Party show up in the Democratic base as well. Ron Brownstein notes in *National Journal* that the top 25 cities that benefit from trade are solidly Democratic. His term "coalition of the ascendant" (minorities, the young, single women, affluent suburbanites) describes the key constituents of today's Democratic Party, while its old base—blue-collar whites—has migrated to the GOP. What this means is that the Republican primaries are more fertile for Trump, or someone with a tough-on-trade message, and Democratic voters may be more receptive to a free-trade message even if union leaders aren't.

Trump's vulnerabilities are obvious, but one that was overlooked in his announcement is that he threatened to raise taxes repeatedly—not income tax rates but tariffs on products from countries that he believes aren't playing fairly with the U.S.

In one example he said that if Ford built a big automotive plant in Mexico rather than the U.S., he would slap a 35 percent tax on cars from that facility entering the U.S. He said the threat would make Ford squirm. The auto behemoth would try to get "President Trump" to change his mind, but it wouldn't work, he predicted.

That's not the same thing as promising to raise taxes, but it's pretty close. If there's anything that unites the diverse strains of the GOP coalition, it's opposition to higher taxes, even if they're import duties. Trump may have opened a door to real electoral opportunity in his announcement by calling for tougher trade policies, but he may have undermined it as well by using the T-word.